Secondhand Success

Darlene Blanchard

Published by Pen and Compass Publishing, 2024.

While every precaution has been taken in the preparation of this book, the publisher assumes no responsibility for errors or omissions, or for damages resulting from the use of the information contained herein.

SECONDHAND SUCCESS

First edition. February 9, 2024.

ISBN: 979-8224970506

Written by Darlene Blanchard.

Forward

A furniture consignment store can be successful in today's for economy for several reasons. Firstly, people become more conscious of their environmental footprint, they are more inclined to buy secondhand or used furniture rather than new. This trend has led to an increased demand for consignment stores that offer high and well-maintained furniture and home décor at affordable prices.

Secondly, the rising popularity of home improvement and interior design shows has made people more interested in decorating and furnishing their homes. Many individuals are constantly looking for unique and stylish pieces that reflect their personal style. Consignment stores provide a broad range of furniture options, allowing customers to find one-of-a-kind items that can't be easily replicated in traditional retail stores.

Up cycling, reducing landfill, being thrifty or a bargain shopper, eco friendly or being green, are all reasons to shop consignment. Other reasons are due to needing an item now, not 6-8 weeks from now and needing to order furniture in advance, as well as seeing and inspecting items in person, versus an online photo.

Consignment buyers will become consignment sellers with consignment sellers becoming consignment buyers once a customer discovers the beauty of consignment furniture. Shoppers rarely go back to paying full retail.

One of the biggest takeaways from this guide is that your furniture consignment business, is that it's truly about solving other people's problems. People needing help liquidating furniture and home decor and those seeking quick fixes for their home environments.

My background includes 45 years experience within retail at every level, from associate to executive and everything in between. I deliberately chose retailers to align myself with so I could learn how each of these businesses gained ground, trained their staff and called the shots to make their goals.

The place where all previous gained knowledge about retail, went out the window, is within the consignment arena.

It's here, in a condensed and concise guide that provides immediate and useful information that can be utilized for a successful business launch of a furniture consignment store. On the surface, an apparent easy business model, however, with many moving parts that include time and motion synchronization.

Your Expenses:

rent/lease

security system

utilities

insurance for store and jewelry*

advertising

phone

POS consignment software

cash register
credit card terminal
banking fees
office desk
filing cabinet
copy machine
computers (3 ,office, jewelry*, sales)
internet
plastic wrap
tagging gun
a few hand tools
measuring tapes
office supplies
cleaning supplies
furniture polish
touch up markers
furniture dolly's
crew t-shirts
payroll
*Should you decide
to include fine jewelry

Imagine, a business model where you don't "need" to purchase inventory! (but it's an option) Just manage what you decide to take in and build relationships with those frequent customers looking for a great deal and problem solve for those just passing through.

CONTENTS

Quick Snapshot
of How It's Done

To set your consignment store apart from others, consider implementing the following strategies:

- **Curate a unique inventory:** Focus on sourcing furniture pieces that have a distinct style or niche appeal. This could include vintage, mid-century modern, or locally handcrafted furniture. By offering a specialized selection, you can attract customers who are specifically looking for those types of items.

- **Build strong relationships with consignors:** Establishing partnerships with reliable consignors who consistently provide high-quality furniture will ensure a steady supply of desirable inventory. This will help differentiate your store from others that may have inconsistent or lower-quality items.

- **Offer additional services:** Consider providing services such as furniture restoration, upholstery, or customization. These value-added services can attract customers who want to personalize or refurbish their furniture. It also helps create a reputation for expertise and quality craftsmanship.

- **Create an inviting and customer-friendly atmosphere:** Ensure your store has an appealing layout, good lighting, and comfortable browsing areas. Invest in knowledgeable staff who can provide personalized assistance and expert advice. Offering exceptional customer service can foster loyalty and encourage word-of-mouth referrals.

- **Embrace digital marketing and online presence:** Utilize social media platforms, online marketplaces, and a user-friendly website to engage with potential customers. With inventory regularly updated, your online platforms will keep customers informed and excited about visiting your store.

By implementing these strategies, you can differentiate your furniture consignment store from competitors and attract customers who value unique, sustainable, and well-crafted furniture.

2
Research and Discovery

Begin by researching the market in your potential business area. Visit a local real estate office or Chamber of Commerce and ask for the demographics of the area. This information is also available online.

Who lives in the area?

What are their ages?

Are there home based worker's, outside the home working couples, stay at home moms?

Long time residents?

Short term residents?

First time home buyers?

What are the style of homes in the area? Tudor, ranch, Spanish, Mediterranean,Colonial,Victorian, Cape Cod, American Craftsman, Farmhouse, Modern, Contemporary, Cottage, French Country, Mission, the list goes on and on.

Apartments, condos, townhomes, lofts, single family residences?

Retirement communities?

Assisted living manor?

AirBnB's?

Vacation homes?

College town with dorms?

Are those in your area, downsizing? Moving?

Would potential college students be short on time and need furniture immediately?

Has your audience gone through a natural disaster or fire?

A family member has passed away and the family wants to liquidate inherited items?

Is the area known for estate sales because garage or yard sales aren't allowed? (Community rules /HOA policy)

Remodeling?

Staging a home for sale?

New home buyers want to get rid of furniture that came with their new home?

Newly divorced?

Determine the demand for furniture consignment after you assess your target audience.

3

Get It On Paper

A business plan is a hypothetical, educated, guesstimate. You can create a business plan outlining your goals, target market, financial projections, marketing strategies, with all the variables plugged in, to assist with keeping you focused and guide you in decision making.

There is ample information available online on how to compile a business plan.

4

Legal Considerations

Register your business and choose a suitable legal structure, such as a sole proprietorship, partnership, LLC or Incorporation.

Obtain any necessary permits or licenses and insurance required by your state or local authorities. Consult with an attorney to ensure compliance with all legal requirements.

Here too, there is ample information and guidance on selecting a business structure, online.

5

Location-Space-Competition

After finding a suitable location: Consider factors like foot traffic, parking availability, and competitors in the area. Ensure that the space is adequate for displaying and storing furniture ready to be picked up or delivered. Ample ceiling height to accommodate unusual items, patio umbrellas and chandeliers, double doors or roll up doors for ease of large furniture coming and going. Cement floors are a must as furniture will be in constant motion.

If you plan on working with furniture manufacturers or wholesalers, delivery trucks may not have a lift gate on their truck as they are used to backing into loading docks. If you don't have a loading dock, you will need movers on staff to off load boxed furniture, an area to house boxed items and an area to un-box and assemble items.

Selecting the right space: If you need a guideline, a 9000 sqft space can typically house a combined 800 pieces of furniture, art and home decor, with an average dollar per square foot of $250.

Consignment competitors: Any competition in close proximity would not be ideal unless the competition has a micro-target, for example,"Mid-Century Modern Furniture", and you opt to stay clear of that design aesthetic. Otherwise, multiple consignment stores in close proximity will end up impacting each others business and no one wins.

Consignment stores near destination locations, such as big box stores, Costco, grocery stores or near a furniture row /district will likely provide higher foot traffic.

6

What Will You Take In?
Quality-Condition-Demand

Reach out to individuals through Craigslist, Facebook Marketplace and by visiting estate sales. You are not buying furniture, only introducing the idea of consignment. Consignment will appeal to potential customers, as after experiencing the DIY way of liquidation, the project may be best turned over to those that can provide insight as to what will move quickly, the right price to sell it for and have the avenue in which to help get the items delivered.

To start, it may be best to take in a little of everything, testing the waters, seeing what your quick selling items are vs. the ones that may take a bit longer to sell. (longer than 30 days).

Take in items that are of excellent quality, in good condition and in demand. Taking in items that are in so-so condition sets a precedent that items you sell, are just that, so-so.
Refurbishing items yourself is a cost you don't want to take on, unless it's replacing simple hardware or allowing slight nicks and scratches that can be addressed with a furniture touch up marker. Factors that will affect pricing will be condition, age, brand and style.

Customers that email images or show you photos on their phone, be mindful of what you see in the background of the pictures, as there are tell tale signs of the potential condition of the items, the era or decade of the rest of the home, and you having any further interest in anything.

It is difficult to see pet hair, sun damage, wobbly legs, missing hardware, or tell if item has been in a smokers home from photos or if a cat has sprayed a corner of the furniture. You'll need to ask questions to assist in determining if the item is a good fit for your store. Ask for the backstory on items. Many times you'll find out that the item was purchased used or was a hand me down, or the item just needs to be gone because the new one is being delivered next week.

Be wary of items having been kept in storage. Storage dries out wood and if it's been in storage for many years, it's likely outdated.

Another tip for taking in items, most people do not want to purchase items that they grew up with or saw at grandmas house. Considered kitschy, vintage, retro or antique these days, items from yesteryear, take longer to move.

On the flip side of the aforementioned, take into consideration what part of the nation or world you intend to do business in. East coast transplants to the west coast, still prefer a traditional aesthetic and may seek items from yesteryear, so it's a crap shoot.

Many times a consignor will suggest, "All someone needs to do is _________" . Enter any of the following: clean it, get it reupholstered, have it refinished,replace the glass, etc. Most purchasers do not want a project and want the item to be functional as soon as it's brought home and put in its space. You don't want a project either.

You will also need to decide if you will take in IKEA type furniture. Typically knock down furniture does not dismantle and go back together very well, MDF or press board are not a favorite of those seeking quality fabrication.

Those that approach you to consign, typically have an issue of needing to get rid of something and:

- Don't know where to start
- Don't have the time to be their own project manager for the task of liquidating
- Don't want strangers in their home
- Don't live in the area and have limited time to clear out the entire house
- Are a project manager or real estate agent trying to assist in disposing of furniture for their client
Should you be approached by a potential customer and shown many photos of furniture in the home, make an appointment to go to the home and see items in person. Home visits expedite the process of items being priced, the customer agreeing to your proposed pricing, having the items picked up and placed in your store.

Those moving or have sold their home may have a MLS (an acronym used in real estate that stands for multiple listing service) link and their home listed on a property for sale site. Ask for the home address and view the interior of the home this way, to either put together a proposal or arrange for a pick up with pricing to be done upon arrival. It's not uncommon to take in items this way as home sellers have other tasks to complete and having furniture and home decor picked up for consignment, is helpful.

Additional avenues to consider as complimentary offerings to your inventory assortment would be designer handbags and fine jewelry.

Designer handbag verification can be done using the Entrupy app which has 99.1% accuracy. This is the same company that certifies authenticity for EBay, ShopGoodwill, OfferUp, Facebook Marketplace and Shopify. It is a subscription service that has tiered pricing for the number of handbags you will potentially take in per month.

Handbags would require locked display cases to showcase inventory. Consignment split does not need to be 50/50. A 60/40 split would be more enticing for a potential consignor.

Fine jewelry consignment would require a GIA (Gemological Institute of America) certified associate to qualify potential consignments. Locked display cases would be needed as well as a floor mounted safe, area alarm, computer and separate insurance. A 60/40 consignment split for fine jewelry is a common split.

Leasing out a designated amount of real estate to a professional jeweler would be an ideal solution and beneficial to your store. There are two ways that your store could be profitable from including fine jewelry:

Charge the jeweler a flat fee per month to operate their business, plus 10% of sales.

Or

20% of the jewelry counters monthly sales.

13

7
How To Price Items

Those in the market for a particular item, know current retail pricing for new items. When they shop consignment they see the savings and appreciate the value pricing on gently loved items.

When potential consignment customers tell you what their gently loved item currently sells for, keep in mind that most customers doing research prior to walking in to your store will gravitate to the highest figure they've come across on the internet. There will also be those that will show you the original receipt of what the item was purchased for. Both customers wanting to get top dollar for their item. Reinforce that YOU set prices based on what the market will bear and that you are partners in consignment. You too want to get the highest price for the item but it needs to be realistic. Review their research and then do your own.

There is a difference when pricing off brand, no name and mass produced items and items that have been custom made, name brand and designer items.
It's a good practice to maintain the value of higher end items, as shoppers may already be shopper savvy and know the true retail value.

Pricing items is an art. Price items too high and it will take forever to move, price items just right and it's sold. You are not an appraiser, just someone that will help liquidate items quickly.

Pricing items too low, also causes a dilemma. Should you have eight dining chairs on your floor at $39 each, ($312 total) you could have taken in a used leather loveseat and sold it for $649-$699, so be careful what you give real estate to.

No need to research every single item that comes through the door. You will decide what price a basic used lamp will sell for. Same with used dining chairs. There will be standard pricing that will become your norm.

Photos being sent to your email address for viewing are potential customers wanting to know how much the item would likely sell for at your store. It is best to provide a range, for example, $129-$179 and explain that the range is conservative since you can't see quality or condition through a photo. Once the item is brought in, if you believe you can get more for the item, raise the asking price.

Side note here in regard to replying to potential consignors that have sent photos for you to consider. Your email signature should include a disclaimer: "It is difficult to see quality and condition through images. We do our best to determine price ranges for your items based on the information you provide. Your item may be declined upon viewing in person."

A quick pricing formula: For new, never used items, right out of a box, price these items at 50% of retail. Even less if the color, style, silhouette, finish, detailing is off trend and only if you believe you can move the item at a reduced price, otherwise, don't invest in giving this item space in your store. New-ish (used once or twice or only a few months) price these items, at 60-75% off of full retail.

Quick cheat sheet: (ranges)

Dresser $179-$499
Chest $179-$279
Nightstand $69-$169
Complete bed $199-499
Headboard only $79-$349
Sofa $399-$899
Loveseat $199-$499
Sofa sleeper $399-$899
Sectional $699-$1299
Dining set $599-$799
China hutch $199-$249
Kitchenette $249-$499
Bookcase $99-$249
Armoire $99-$249
Accent chair $99-$499
Recliner $199-$599
Coffee table $99-$399
End table $49-$199
Media cabinet $99-$279
Console $99-$399
*Piano $399-13,000
Art $29-$20,000
Lamps $19-$199
Chandeliers $49-$399
Decorator pillows $19-$49

Ranges include variables such as upholstery vs. leather, foam filled vs. down filled, furniture with USB ports, exotic wood, brand name vs. off brand, manual vs. electric.

*Side note: Upright pianos do not need specialized movers. Upright pianos can be moved by furniture delivery companies. Grand and baby grand pianos need specialized piano movers.

8
The Consignment Agreement
& Store Policies

Develop clear and comprehensive consignment agreements for your business. Your consignment agreement should outline the terms and conditions for accepting furniture from consignors, including pricing, commission rates, payment terms, and return policies.

Provide a pamphlet with your store consignment terms and store policies for walk in inquiries and again, printed on the contract that new consignors signs.

Consignment Policy Examples

Length of a consignment contract is typically a 45 to 60 day maximum duration.

- "We" (insert business name) set the selling price.

- The consignor agrees that he/she is the rightful owner or is legally entitled to sell the items/place items on consignment.

- New purchasers of your item will not be called on your behalf should you change your mind and want your item back. This includes wanting to retrieve your sold consigned item because your sister said she now wants the item you placed on consignment.

- Consignor is to receive 50% (or what you have determined for your business) of net proceeds. Net proceeds to include deductions for credit card service fees. (or check verification fee's should you decide to take personal checks)

- Selling price is subject to automatic permission to reduce your item up to 20%, at any time. Any reduction more than 20% of then current asking price requires consignors approval. Telephone approval is acceptable.

(Best to make notes on customers account each and every time the customer calls in to check on their items or if you have called them to seek a price reduction greater than 20%.)

- Consignor can cancel and remove any item from selling floor prior to the contract ending, provided there is no pending sale. Removal of your item may be subject to an administrative fee of 15% of original asking price.

- Consignment earnings will be processed within 30 days of the sale. Checks will be mailed to the address on file. It is up to the consignor to maintain a current mailing address. Inventory numbers assigned to your consigned items on your your original contract will be referenced in the memo section of your check. (or on a separate document)

- Consignor will be charged a processing fee of $___ that will be deducted from each issued check.

- If after 30 days that an item is not likely to sell, consignor agrees to reduce current price, donate, or pick up item as suggested. If items are not picked up after 3 months from original consignment date, and multiple documented attempts to contact consignor, consignor agrees that ownership of your item transfers to us. (make a note under the customers account each time you have left a message for the consignor to pick up their item)

- If item has not sold and customer has been notified to pick item up, it must be picked up immediately 3-7 days, or it will be donated and customer will receive a tax donation form.

Store Policy Examples

- We provide complementary storage after a purchase, up to 7 days. Purchasers not picking up their items after 7 days are subject to storage fees of $5.00 per day, per item. Items will be released after payment is received.

- Items paid for by personal check are subject to a five business day waiting period, allowing for check clearance, before items will be released for pick up or delivery. (or you can decide not to take personal checks at all)

- Item is not allowed to be advertised on social media for sale at a higher price while it is under contract with us. Violators will forfeit consigning again and your item/s must be removed from the store immediately.

- Images viewed by emailed photos or on a cell phone for potential consignment are subject to being declined upon arrival.

- Consignor agrees that to the best of his/her knowledge, items are as represented; clean, smoke free, no pet hair, no wobbly legs, no missing hardware, cracked, stained, sun faded, cushions have good return, chairs that have not bottomed out.

- If you failed to measure correctly and the item you purchased doesn't fit through the doorway, is too large for the room or can't make the turn going up the stairs, we will consider reconsigning the item. Refer to our store policy regarding all sales are final.

- You may place an item on a 24 hour hold. Maximum of three items. Items must be $100+ each, not a total of $100

- We allow you to try it before you buy it. Take an item home to see if it works. We reserve the right to decline the try it before you buy it on items sensitive to being handled incorrectly. (white loveseat being moved by your son and next door neighbor, the item may not come back in the same condition it left in) We pre-authorize the entire amount of the item on a credit card and you take the item home to see if it works. If it doesn't work, return the item within the 24 hour period. You won't be charged. If you miss the 24 hour window, you now own the item.

- You can't combine a 24 hour hold and a 24 hour, try it before you buy it.

- If you place an item on a 24 hour hold, you are agreeing to the full selling price.

- You can not receive a verbal discount and then put an item on hold, then return to the store and argue about being told you were given a discount.

- Your 24 hour hold expires at the close of the following day.

- All sales are final

A Word About Discounts

There are no good reasons to discount items if you have already value priced the item and can verify that the current selling price is lower or in line with what the item can be found for elsewhere. The exception would be, if the item is no longer a wanted item, help it out the door by providing incentive to move it quick, give a discount to the next interested purchaser. If you find yourself and your staff constantly selling items at a discount, you may want to evaluate the way you are setting item pricing, as well as reviewing the taking in off items that are being discounted.

Many conversations that arise on the sales floor will be in regard to discounts. "If I purchase many items, what kind of discount can I get?", "If I pay cash, what kind of discount can I get?", "This item has some damage, what kind of discount can I get?", "When do you discount items in the store?", "Can you not charge me tax?", "I know this item just came in, but what kind of discount can you give me?"

Here are good responses to those scenarios:
"If I purchase many items, what kind of discount can I get?"...We don't own any of this merchandise, it's all owned by different families, there are no bulk discounts, however, I can check to see if anything is eligible for a discount.

"If I pay cash, what kind of discount can I get?"...Unfortunately, there are no discounts for paying cash, but I will check to see if anything is eligible for a discount.

"This item has some damage, what kind of discount can I get?"...If it was perfect, it'd be more expensive. (This retort is a bit snarky, but it address's the haggling immediately) When pricing this item, we took the condition into consideration. Let's find something else within your budget and remember, these items are gently used, pre-loved.

"When do you discount items in the store?"...We value price items and know they need to be lower than anything else you can find elsewhere. We will consider discounting an item if it is no longer a desired item, stopped trending or we've made the wrong choice to include it in our inventory. We will evaluate items after three weeks of being on the floor.

"Can you not charge me tax?"...Unfortunately, we pay tax, so you must pay tax, unless you're a re-seller.

"I know this item just came in, but what kind of discount can you give me?"...We don't bring in items just to discount them the following day. We give items a chance to sell at the set price. If the item is still in inventory after 3 weeks, we can re-visit providing a discount. We are advocates for the family that has consigned with us and represent them. Know that if you were to consign with us, we wouldn't discount your item the day after it arrived.

9
Working With Re-Sellers

You may have re-sellers purchase from you and want to use their registered business to bypass paying state tax.
(your POS software program will be able to accommodate not charging state tax to re-sellers)

Many times, consignment pricing is attractive to re-sellers. There could be enough wiggle room for a re-seller to increase the selling price up to three times as much to their specific audience and they will frequent your business seeking treasures.

Get to know your re-sellers and call them when any of the items they seek come into your store. Keep a running "Wish Book" with customers names and telephone numbers along with a description of what they are seeking.

10
Buying Merchandise From
Bankrupt Manufacturers,
Close Out Liquidators & Wholesalers

Manufacturers, liquidators and wholesalers are always seeking new avenues of distribution. It is likely that you would need to take in multiples of the same item, which would give your store a different appearance and even lose its original appeal. It is also likely that you would "pay" for these items at a reduced price, making it attractive to make your money back quickly. Bankrupt furniture companies are in different situations and their offering would be more interesting. Items could be sold to you as low as $50 per box. In those boxes could be recliners, accent chairs or dressers.

Keep your ears open, keep tabs on business closing's. Don't shy away from items you've never carried before. Make a call to see where he firm is at in the liquidation process. You may discover that they may be very willing to negotiate with you.

11
Hiring Your Staff

Those with a background in furniture sales, art history, interior decorators, woodworkers, antique dealers and those with a flair for home fashions are good choices as crew members. What your staff doesn't know, can be taught. You can also rely on peer-to-peer training as well.
(Use 15 minutes prior to store opening to review the names of furniture, textiles and finishes)

The important aspect of having the right team members is their ability to learn the consignment business and develop a comfort level with determining selling prices and declining items that your store will have trouble selling.

Should you decide to go out on home visits, having a well seasoned and able crew at the store will be needed in your absence.

Side note: Should your staff begin to visit customers homes to view potential items for consignment, be informed about state laws that require employers to reimburse employees for mileage and the use of personal technology. (cell phones and tablets)
Almost every state has a law regarding reimbursement for personal cell phone usage the use of personal cell phone for work related tasks.

12

In-House Movers

It would be beneficial to have two to three in house movers on staff at all times. Walk in customers will have items in their vehicles, hoping to consign. Movers will off load these items as well as carry out newly purchased items.

For liability purposes, it would be recommended that movers can carry out and load a vehicle for a customer, but don't allow your movers to tie down products. Carry outs and loading is a courtesy and these are movers, not a delivery company.

Charge a fee if a customer wants items wrapped in plastic after purchase. (a furniture delivery company will include wrapping with their fee) Rent furniture blankets to customers, picking up their own furniture, on a cash only basis to ensure the return of your blanket.

Have the delivery company you'll be contracting, train your crew to lift correctly.

13

Partner With a Delivery Company

Customers may ask if you can provide local or regional deliveries. It would be in the best interest of business to locate a licensed, bonded and insured delivery company to provide this service.

You would want to coordinate the pick up at your store for the customer. (By providing this service, it allows you to keep a sharp eye on the movement of furniture and available real estate for saying yes to new arrivals.) Ask the customer for two options of when they can meet the delivery company and then call the delivery company to see if they can deliver around one of the two options.

Before the grand opening of your store, locate a reputable delivery company and negotiate a delivery rate for your customers. Typically, with giving the delivery company so much new business, your rates would likely be lower than what the customer could get on their own.

It is best to have customers pay the delivery company upon arrival. Don't handle this fee yourself. The delivery company will likely already be set up to take cash,Venmo, Zelle or Apple Pay.

You would also use this delivery company to pick up items from home visits too. The delivery company now has two streams of income from your business; deliveries and home pick-ups.

The delivery company will need a manifest/list of items that they are picking up and/or delivering.

When delivering, a copy of the store receipt/s works well to hand off to the delivery company. When picking up, it is up to you to provide the delivery company a manifest/ list of what they are to pick up. Customers sometimes take advantage of placing items on the delivery truck that you never saw during your home visit or didn't agree to consign. It leaves the delivery company in an awkward position of saying yes or no to a customer.

The most challenging aspect of logistics will be anticipating the available space on the delivery truck. Many times, the delivery company will want to view a list/manifest of the items to be picked up from the store or customers home, to allow them to plan for the correct vehicle and staffing. Some pick ups only need a cargo van, other pick ups or deliveries require a truck with a lift gate. As a courtesy, allows advise the delivery company you are working with about items that need extra care, or are extremely heavy or in awkward locations. Many times, the delivery company will be your eyes out in the field and will call you if something doesn't look right and will alert you to help make a decision on transporting the item/s. Concrete coffee tables are transportable, however, it may be very difficult for your in-house crew of two, to move this concrete coffee table when it took a crew of four to bring it to your store.

Keep two active files:

One for all furniture to be delivered and another for all the furniture to picked up. Purge these files on a daily basis.

14

Partner With a Donation Center

Find a charity shop, Salvation Army, Goodwill, or donation center that is nearby. Make arrangements with the owner or manager to take in salable items that your customers have agreed to donate / have declined to pick up after their contract with you has ended. Many times these organizations have their own truck and can pick up items quickly and at no cost.

It is up to you to track the items being sent to donation and ensure that the customer receives a tax donation form for their charitable donation. (make a note on the customer's account and also keep a file of every item sent to donation for the month) Work with the owner or manager to determine if the organization or you will forward a tax donation form.

15

Marketing, Advertising & Promotion

Develop a marketing strategy to attract customers to your consignment business. Utilize online platforms, social media, local advertising, and networking to raise awareness about your store. Offer promotions, or loyalty programs to entice repeat customers. Be aware that you can not reduce the selling price of items of private consignors without consulting the consignor first.

16

Daily Operations

In a nutshell, establish effective inventory management systems, pricing strategies, and customer service practices. Train your staff on proper handling of furniture, customer interactions, and sale techniques. Evaluate slow selling items, follow up on holds that have expired to see if there is still interest in the item.

Consignment furniture should be regularly monitored on the floor to ensure that it continues to attract potential buyers and doesn't remain stagnant. Here are a few steps to determine whether an item needs to be marked down or returned to the consignor:

- **Evaluate the time it has been on the floor:** Take note of how long the furniture piece has been displayed. If it has been sitting for a significant amount of time without any interest or inquiries, it may be a sign that it needs to be marked down.

- **Compare pricing and market demand:** Research similar items in the market and compare their prices. If you consignment furniture is priced higher than its competitors or there is low demand for that particular style, it might be necessary to consider marking it down.

What the sales staff should be doing on a daily basis:

Opening the Store:

- Arrive early to ensure the store is clean and tidy before opening.
- Turn on lights, open doors, and prepare the cash register for the day.
- Check inventory levels and restock any items that are running low.
- Sales associates should study the floor every shift to view what has come and gone.

Organizing and Displaying Furniture:

- Inspect new arrivals and decide on their placement within the store.
- Arrange furniture in an appealing and organized manner to attract customers.
- Dust and clean each item to maintain a presentable appearance.

Customer Assistance:

- Greet customers as they enter the store and offer assistance.
- Provide information about different pieces of furniture, their features, and prices.
- Answer customer inquiries regarding consignment terms, returns, and warranties.

Sales and Payment Processing:

- Assist customers in making purchasing decisions and provide any necessary measurements or details.
- Process sales transactions accurately using the cash register or point-of-sale system.
- Accept various payment methods such as cash, credit cards, or mobile payments.
- Provide measuring tapes for customers to take dimensions. By providing measuring tapes, it's a great sales technique to assist customers in taking dimensions and learn what they are shopping for. Measuring tapes are ice breakers.
- Your sales team should be in the habit of referring to the Wish Book to see if any customers or re-sellers can be called and informed of items that may fit their request.

Consignment Intake and Pricing:

- Evaluate furniture brought in by consignors and determine its market value.
- Negotiate pricing with consignors based on store policies.
- Properly document consignment agreements and track inventory in the store's system.

Merchandising and Promotions:

- Create attractive displays that showcase furniture pieces and highlight unique features.
- Design promotional materials or signs to draw attention to sales or discounts.
- Collaborate with marketing teams to develop strategies for reaching a wider audience.
- Oversee social media platforms.(typically the owner/ manager should oversee the final social media content before posting)

Inventory Management:

- Monitor inventory levels, noting which items are selling well and which need more marketing.
- Replenish stock from the backroom or storage area as needed.
- Regularly update the store's inventory system to reflect

sold items and new arrivals.

Closing the Store:

- Tidy up the store, ensuring furniture is neatly arranged and all areas are clean. Including outside dumpsters and surrounding area.
- Secure cash register and complete end-of-day financial procedures. Refill ink, paper, register receipt tape. Communicate with next day crew of any follow up information or "To-Do" list.
- Lock up the store, ensuring all doors and windows are properly secured.

Keep The Consignor Informed

Communicate with the consignor: If you believe the furniture is not selling well or needs to be marked down, it's essential to have open communication with the consignor. Discuss the situation, explain your observations, and seek their input. They may decide to reduce the price or choose to retrieve the item.

Remember, proper documentation and clear communication with the consignor throughout this monitoring process is vital to maintain a positive relationship and ensure a successful consignment business.

There are several indicators or signs that suggest an item of consignment needs to be marked down or returned to the consignor.

Lack of interest or slow sales: If an item has been on the sales floor for a considerable amount of time without generating much interest or sales, it may be a sign that it is priced too high or not appealing to customers.

Condition issues: If an item shows significant wear and tear, damage, or other condition issues that were not properly disclosed, misrepresented or noticed at the time of consignment, it may need to be marked down or returned to the consignor. This includes strong odors; furniture with persistent smells such as smoke, pet urine, or mildew will not sell and an immediate call to the consignor made and items need to be picked up at their expense.

Outdated style or trend: Furniture trends change over time, and if an item is outdated or no longer in style, it may be difficult to sell at the original price. In such cases, marking it down or returning it to the consignor could be a better option.

Overstocked inventory: If your store is facing an excess of inventory or limited space, you may need to evaluate which items are not selling well and consider marking them down or returning them to the consignor to make room for new consignments.

Remember, it's crucial to establish clear guidelines and policies regarding marking down or returning consignment items to ensure fairness and consistency in your consignment business. Regular monitoring, assessment, and open communication with the consignor will help you make informed decisions in these situations.

Identify Status Of Items
On The Sales Floor

Identifying sold products on your floor is best done by color coding **SOLD** tags for viewing at a glance.

SOLD tags can be the size of a large index card. Information on all SOLD tags should include spaces for:

Date sold
Date being picked up
Sales Associate initials
Customers last name
Inventory number
Item description
Special instructions

(for privacy, never a customers phone number)

RED Sold tags- customer is picking up items themselves

GREEN Sold tags- customers wanting the delivery company to pick up

Donate tag-make this tag **BLUE** Attach the customers name and address on the item, in an envelope for privacy, so that the organization knows where to mail the tax donation form. Be sure to remove this item from your inventory data base.

Consignor Pick Up-make this tag **YELLOW** Have a space for the customers name, description of the item and a place for the date it is to be picked up. Be sure to remove this item from your inventory data base.

HOLD tags, make this tag **PINK**. This tag can be a smaller size, the size of a drivers license. Space for customers last name, inventory number, date and sales associate initials. (keep customers telephone number on file under the items inventory number and not on the HOLD tag for privacy reasons)

You will need to monitor the coming and going of furniture on your floor to know when you can accept furniture without being in danger of breaking fire regulations and ADA laws. (three foot aisles, electrical boxes not blocked, etc.) Saying yes to three full 3000 sqft homes in one week, along with walk-in customers and your regular inventory, could have you at capacity in a short time.

19

Store Layout, Design, Merchandising

Create an inviting and appealing store layout. The racetrack, maze or free flow, floor plan works well for consignment stores. Arrange furniture in an organized manner and use creative displays to showcase your inventory. Design a comfortable and visually appealing shopping environment.

Refrain from merchandising all alike categories in designated areas. There is nothing more unappealing than viewing dressers, nightstands and bookcases lined up like soldiers. The magic happens when your staff can apply their talents to arrange and dress small vignettes in your store to make each item shine.

Showcase curated collections. Consignment stores can create curated collections inspired by popular home improvement and interior design shows. By featuring furniture pieces that resemble those seen on TV, customers will feel like they're bringing a touch of their favorite shows into their homes.

Host events and workshops. Organize events and workshops related to home improvement and interior design. Invite local experts to give talks on the latest trends, design tips, and DIY projects. This will create a sense of community around your store and position it as a go-to destination for all things related to home improvement and interior design.

Utilize social media platforms. Share regular updates on your store's social media platforms, showcasing furniture pieces similar to what viewers may have seen on TV. Engage with your audience by encouraging them to share their own home improvement and interior design projects. This will create a sense of connection and encourage customers to visit your store.

Replicate room setups. Take inspiration from the rooms featured in popular magazines and recreate similar setups in your store. Use matching furniture pieces, accessories, and décor to create a cohesive look that reflects the style of the what has been featured in print.

Use trendy colors and patterns. Pay attention to the color schemes and patterns used in popular tv shows and incorporate them into your displays. This will help create a visually appealing and trendy atmosphere that resonates with customers.

Showcase statement pieces. Home improvement shows often highlight statement pieces that catch the viewer's attention. Include eye-catching furniture items or accessories in your displays to draw customers in and make your store stand out.

Create themed displays. Take inspiration from specific design styles or trends showcased in popular shows and create themed displays in your store. For example, you could create a display focused on rustic farmhouse decor or a display inspired by tropical vibes.

Incorporate technology. Consider incorporating digital displays, interactive touch screens, or virtual reality experiences to enhance your displays and engage customers. Prop an ipad nearby with a looped video of someone playing the piano you just consigned.

Incorporate visual elements. Use visually appealing props, such as rugs, curtains, or wallpaper, to create a more immersive experience for customers. This can help them envision how certain pieces of furniture would look in their own homes.

Use lighting effectively. Lighting plays a crucial role in interior design, so make sure to highlight the furniture pieces in your store with appropriate lighting. Experiment with different lighting fixtures and techniques to create a warm and inviting atmosphere.

Showcase before and after transformations. Many home improvement shows focus on transforming spaces. You could incorporate before and after photos from real-life customer projects to showcase the potential of your furniture pieces in creating stunning makeovers.

Collaborate with local designers. Partner with local interior designers or decorators to create vignette displays on your store floor that reflect their unique styles. This not only adds variety to your displays but also helps build valuable connections within the design community.

Offer design consultations. Set up a designated space in your store where customers can schedule design consultations with experts. This personalized service adds value to their shopping experience and helps them envision how certain furniture pieces could fit into their homes.

Mix and match styles. Many home improvement shows feature a blend of different styles, such as modern, industrial, or bohemian. Experiment with mixing and matching different furniture pieces and styles in your displays to create a unique and eclectic look.

Remember, the key is to create an inviting and inspiring shopping environment and that will keep customers engaged.

20

Website and Online Presence

Build a user-friendly website where customers can browse the categories you will take in. (carpets and baby cribs seem to be problem items that many consignment stores won't take in) Include details on how consignment works, home visits are available if you have more than 10 items, what your split is, etc. Optimize your website for search engines to improve your online visibility.

Include an email address where potential consignors can send photos of items for consignment consideration.

Facebook, Instagram and TicToc are social media platforms that should be used to announce new items, highlight unusual items or showcase a bit of design expertise or a relatable story you develop.

21

Networking and Partnerships

Establish relationships with local interior designers, home staging companies, real estate agents, and other businesses that may refer customers to your store.

Collaborate with influencer's. Partner with influencer's who are interested in home improvement, interior design and those influencer's of certain aesthetics. Invite these influencer's to visit your store, feature your furniture pieces on their social media platforms, and provide recommendations to their followers. This exposure can help increase your store's visibility and attract new customers.

Consider hosting events. Events will attract potential customers and build connections within the industry. Another approach specifically for real estate agents would be to make a presentation to the local or regional office for all agents in the area.

Assisted living facilities. Seek out the local assisted living facilities in your area that have directories for families, of local businesses, that provide specialty services. Usually, being listed in this directory is free.

Pop-Up location. This could be an interesting idea to participate in a satellite location as a unique offering to the community you wouldn't normally reach. "The Great American

Junk Hunt" is a traveling, three day event for those seeking unique items. This could be worth looking into.

Contests. Invite customers to submit before and after images of how purchasing items from your store transformed their project.

22

Point Of Sale System

Here's a starting point on researching software for your POS. Most programs are customizable should you want something special to be tracked or noted.

PayGoPOS
ConsignPro
ConsignCloud
SimpleConsign

As a successful business owner of a furniture consignment store it is important to have a software system in place that caters to the specific needs of your business. Here are some key information and criteria that should be included in the software and why they are important: Inventory management.

The software you should have for your consignment store, you'd want to consider including an inventory management system with the following information that allows you to track and manage all the inventory for your store:

Look for a system that has features that allow you to record item descriptions, pricing, the ability to track length of time item has been in inventory, condition, furniture measurements, stock levels, markdown, special instructions and any other relevant information you may want to include.

The software should also include contact details for the consignor, payment history, items that have been picked up or donated. A system that tracks sales and generates accurate and timely payments and reports for analysis.

Automated reminders for contract expiration, notification of payment due dates, and overdue alerts are also beneficial for maintaining turn over of inventory.

Sales and reporting should provide details like the item sold, sale price, and commission owed to the consignor.

Software that includes marketing and promotions capabilities could help manage marketing campaigns and promotions by allowing you to create targeted customer lists, track response rates, and measure the effectiveness of different strategies.

Integrating your POS system with online platforms is a wonderful option. In today's digital world, having an online presence is crucial for any business. The software should have features that enable you to manage an e-commerce website in real time.

Overall, having a software system tailored to your furniture consignment store can greatly enhance operational efficiency, increase sales potential, and provide valuable insights into your business.

Investing in a comprehensive and user-friendly software solution will ultimately save time, reduce errors, and improve customer satisfaction. expands your reach and provides added convenience for customers.

Finally, reporting and analytics helps you identify trends, sales performance and make data-driven decisions, with the software able to generate reports on sales, consignor activity, inventory turnover, and assist you with continuously improving your store's performance.

By implementing a software solution that encompasses these essential features, you can streamline operations, enhance efficiency, and ultimately drive the success of your furniture consignment store.

It is beneficial if the software has a mobile app or a responsive web interface, allowing you to access and manage your consignment store's operations from anywhere.

Yes, the right software can generate reports, analyze sales data to identify top-selling items, average customer spending and overall profitability. You can also track trends over time, such as which

types of furniture are in high demand or which months hav
the highest sales. These insights can help you make informe
decisions about inventory management, pricing strategies, an
marketing campaigns.

Some software includes the ability for customers to purchas
items with a payment plan / lay-way option. (an interestin
offering for high ticket items) This is paying for a purchase ove
time and when the items are paid for in full, items can then b
picked up. Your service and layaway agreement would need to b
air tight to ensure that purchasers are bound to respecting you
terms.

23

Get Organized

Now that you've digested the concepts and how-to's of startin
your own furniture consignment and home décor consignmen
business, let's prioritize the next steps of making things happen.

You will be juggling a few segments of the busines
simultaneously, as one business topic will be contingent upo
the other, so understand this going in.

Find the location:
-Research potential locations
-Consider the activity within the city and your audience
-Look into zoning laws and regulations (delivery trucks comin
and going, dumpster availability, hours of operations

-Negotiate lease terms

Choose a business structure:
-Register your business with the appropriate government agencies
-Obtain any necessary licenses or permits

Develop a website:
-Design a user-freindly website
-Include information about consignment and how it works
-Implement ecommerce functionality if you decide to sell items from your website

Get insurance:
-Research differnet types of business insurance (general liability, property, workers' compensation, etc.)
-Obtain insurance quotes from multiple providers

Set up utilities:
-Contact utilities providers (electricity, water, gas, internet, store alarm) to set up accounts
-Determine if you will have a write in time card system for your associates or electronic time card system
-Ensure all utilities are connected before opening

Open up a bank account:
-Shop financial institutions to determine what their offerings are
-Provide documentation (business registration, personal identification, etc.)

-Set up online banking

-Set up payment processing system (be able to accept credit cards)

Advertise for sales associates and in-house movers:

-Create job postings for all positions, with hourly wage range

-Conduct interviews and hire staff

-Complete I9 form and perform background checks for potential new hires (independent firms do background checks for a minimal fee)

-Provide training for your team

Secure inventory prior to store opening:

-Contact real estate agents

-Contact home stagers

-Contact assisted living facilities

-Contact those with items for sale at estate sales, Facebook Marketplace, Craigslist, etc.

Point-Of-Sale:

-Purchase computers and research the software

-Purchase ticket printer for inventory control

Printing & Advertising:

-Place advertisements where you see fit

-Place your order for letterhead, invoices, contracts, business cards, signs, in-house mover tshirts, etc.

Employee Handbook

It would be to your advantage to develop a comprehensive employee handbook for your staff. An employee handbook would provide detailed information and direction on topics important to you and the team you will employ.

Here are topics to include:

-Introduction and welcome message

-Company policies and procedures

-Job duties and responsibilities (you may want to develop an employee handbook for sales associates and another for your in-house movers as there will be different requirements for your in-house movers and would cover, safe lifting, working in tandem to carry and move furniture to customers vehicles, off loading a delivery truck, etc.)

-Work schedules (what are part-time hours, what are full time hours, shift start and end times),holidays that the business is closed, paid holidays, etc.

-Attendance requirements (being on time, not showing up without calling, etc.)

-Compensation and benefits

-Code of conduct and workplace behavior

-Safety guidelines

-Emergency procedures

-Dress code, personal appearance and personal hygiene

-Performance expectations and evaluation process

-Employee development and training opportunities

-Disciplinary actions and grievance procedures

-Equal employment opportunity and anti-discrimination policies

-Reimbursement for mileage and use of personal cell phone

-Confidentiality and data security measures

-Open door policy to share issues or concerns (provide a telephone number or alternative email address to allow associates direct contact with owner/manager as another option to communicate when face-to-face discussion isn't a practical option.

By organizing your employee handbook with separate headers for each topic, you can make it easier for your employees to

navigate and reference the information they need. This will help
ensure that everyone is on the same page and aware of their
rights and responsibilities as employees of your business.

25
Conclusion

Stay updated on industry trends, customer preferences, and changing market dynamics. Regularly assess and adapt your business strategies to stay competitive in the market. Learn t adapt your inventory and pricing to the economy.

Starting a furniture consignment store requires careful planning, effective marketing, and providing exceptional customer service. By incorporating these, you can increase your chances of success and create a thriving business.

Remember, these steps may vary depending on the specific policies and procedures of each furniture consignment store. It important for sales staff to have good communication skills, product knowledge, and a friendly attitude to provide excellent customer service and maximize sales opportunities.

It is truly the business of solving other people's problems and you can have fun while doing it.